EXTREME CAREERS

WAR CORRESPONDENTS

Life Under Fire

Magdalena Alagna

the rosen publishing group's
rosen
central

Published in 2003 by The Rosen Publishing Group, Inc.
29 East 21st Street, New York, NY 10010

First Edition

Library of Congress Cataloging-in-Publication Data

Alagna, Magdalena.
War correspondents : life under fire / by Magdalena Alagna.— 1st ed.
   p. cm. — (Extreme careers)
Includes bibliographical references and index.
ISBN 0-8239-3798-4 (library binding)
1. Journalism—Vocational guidance. 2. War correspondents. I. Title.
II. Series.
PN4797 .A42 2002
070.4'333'023—dc21

                                                           2002007467

Manufactured in the United States of America

Contents

Introduction

Do you have a great need to know what's going on anywhere and everywhere, but especially where the trouble is? Do you have a passion for telling things the way you see them? Does it bother you that so many countries in the world do not have a free press, and that the people living in those countries therefore are not able to tell their own stories? Would you like to help report the truth? According to "War Stories," an essay by Harry Evans, Hiram Johnson, a senator from California, said this famous quote: "The first casualty when war comes is truth." As a war correspondent, your reporting of the events at the scene of a conflict will help to ensure that the truth is told.

Walter Cronkite, whose groundbreaking coverage of the Vietnam War brought the conflict to millions of viewers in the United States and abroad, testifies on Capitol Hill in October 1991 during hearings on news reporting during the Gulf War.

War Correspondents: Life Under Fire

According to *Flash! The Associated Press Covers the World*, television news legend Walter Cronkite described the mission of war correspondents to educate the public about their leaders this way: "We must know what they are doing in our name." As a war correspondent, you may influence the course of history just by being present. Can you think quickly? Do you have a knack for improvising? How would you feel about going into battle—unarmed? As a war correspondent, you will be armed with only your wits, your knack with people, and the tools of your trade: your eyes and ears; a laptop computer; and a satellite hookup to your newspaper, radio station, or television station. As a war correspondent, you go wherever news is happening anywhere around the world.

If you're thinking about a career as a war correspondent, you can forget hotel room service, blow dryers, and the latest movies. Think about putting all of your courage and talent to the test. A career as a war correspondent is nothing less than an adventure. At its best it is a profession in which you provide an important service: making the public aware of what is really happening at the scene of conflict. However, there are substantial risks to the profession. Do you remember the 2002 kidnapping and brutal murder of Daniel Pearl, foreign correspondent with the *Wall Street Journal*? In fact, a total of thirty-seven journalists were killed worldwide as a direct result of their work in 2001, up from twenty-four killed in 2000, according to the Committee to Protect Journalists (CPJ), a nonprofit group that works to protect press freedoms and reporters all over the world. In many countries, journalists are murdered just for doing their jobs.

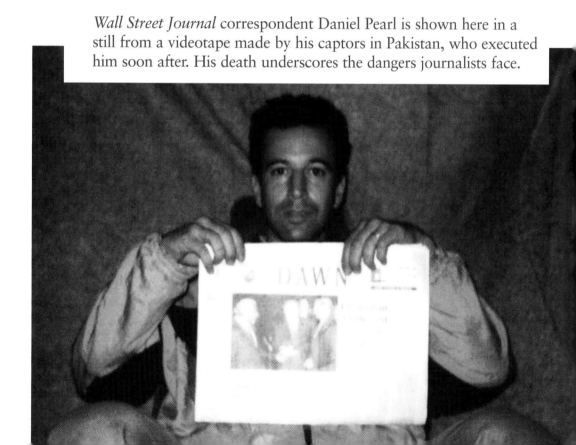

Wall Street Journal correspondent Daniel Pearl is shown here in a still from a videotape made by his captors in Pakistan, who executed him soon after. His death underscores the dangers journalists face.

War Correspondents: Life Under Fire

War correspondents are journalists. Journalists are people who report current events for media such as newspapers, magazines, or radio or television programs. What makes war correspondents different from regular journalists is that they travel very extensively, sometimes relocating for years to the site of the story they're covering. War correspondents, also called war reporters or simply foreign correspondents, do not always have the same sort of glamour that their television news counterparts do. According to a December 13, 2001, article on ABCNews.com, correspondent Ian Stewart, an Associated Press (AP) reporter from Canada who was wounded in Sierra Leone in 1999, said, "It's not glamorous at all. It's miserable. It's a really, really unpleasant existence." However, if you have what it takes to succeed in this job, you won't let a little unpleasantness stop you from uncovering the truth. Consider the feelings of foreign correspondent Hugh A. Mulligan. As reported in *Flash! The Associated Press Covers the World*, Mulligan said as he was leaving for an assignment to cover the war in Vietnam, "Soon I will be in Vietnam again. Another adventure awaits . . . I am engaged in the most exciting profession in the world. I have already seen more sights from better seats than any rich man can afford."

If you are the kind of person who wants a desk job with regular hours, war reporting is definitely not for you. Journalism is a demanding profession. It often involves long, erratic hours. It is possible to make your own hours to some extent if you are going to be a freelance war reporter. Freelancers are not employed by any one agency, such as a television news network, that pays them to cover stories. A freelance reporter gets stories and then sells the stories wherever he or she can, to whichever news media will buy them. Do you need a career that lets you move around a lot and meet a lot of people? Do you get bored doing the same thing day after day? If you like excitement and change, then war correspondence could be for you.

This book will give you an overview of the history of war correspondence. You'll find out what it takes to become a war correspondent, and what you can do right now to prepare yourself for this exciting, dramatic, and important career.

Risky Business 1

War correspondents are journalists who report the news from a battle or the scene of a conflict. The type of news they report is what makes war correspondents different from regular journalists, who report news but are not necessarily at the scene of a battle. The news gets reported in a variety of different ways. Some journalists work in the print media. They write news stories that will be printed in newspapers or magazines. Other journalists write stories that will be read on news radio broadcasts. Some radio stations are devoted entirely to news coverage, while others save just a portion of each hour for news bulletins. There are journalists that write news to be posted on the Internet, either for news Web sites or for news

War correspondents differ from many of the press celebrities with whom we are familiar, such as Larry King *(left)* shown here with President George W. Bush and First Lady Laura Bush.

sections of Internet magazines and newspapers. Other journalists work in television news. These journalists not only come up with the ideas for stories and then write them, they often read the stories on the television news program for which they work.

Whether working full-time for one publication or freelance for several different clients, journalists have certain traits in common. They have a nose for news, meaning they have an instinct for what the reading or viewing public will find important or newsworthy.

They are proactive in their pursuit of a story. A good journalist never lets a story come to him or her. That is the way to get scooped, or have someone else report a story before you do. A good journalist always pursues a story, not the other way around.

Being a war correspondent usually means that you will be living for a time wherever the action is, and not in the town or city that's your home. For instance, you could work for the *New York Times* as a London correspondent and be living in London instead of in New York. A war correspondent does not always have to relocate permanently; however, you should get used to the idea of living away from home and traveling quite a bit if you want to be a war correspondent.

What War Correspondents Do

War correspondents report the events at the scene of a battle or a conflict. How they go about doing this depends on whether they are employed full-time or working freelance. Either way, journalists rely in part on news briefings. News briefings are short statements, either issued aloud or in writing, given by the military and the government to the press. The military informs the media about the conflict, and then war correspondents (who are members of the media) go to the scene of the conflict to report what they see. The military and the media work hand in hand, in a sense. To be a U.S. war correspondent, you must be accredited with the U.S. Department of Defense. This means that you have fulfilled the military's requirements and have filed paperwork so that the military has you registered as an official war correspondent.

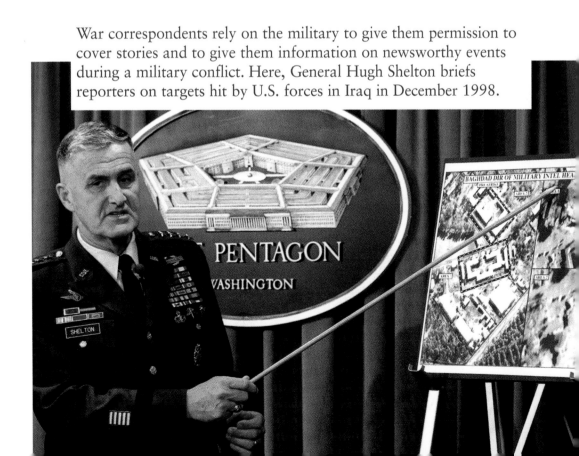

War correspondents rely on the military to give them permission to cover stories and to give them information on newsworthy events during a military conflict. Here, General Hugh Shelton briefs reporters on targets hit by U.S. forces in Iraq in December 1998.

War Correspondents: Life Under Fire

   War correspondents, as do journalists worldwide, act as the watchdogs of government. War correspondents make sure that events are retold in an objective way so that all sides of a situation can be represented. This often means that many people whose rights are being taken away will have a voice when a war reporter covers their story and the story hits the news. When the public becomes aware of situations in which people's rights are being compromised, there is a chance that something can be done to help them. War reporting aims to ensure that crimes do not go unnoticed and, ultimately, uncorrected or unpunished.

   As you can imagine, war reporters report incidents that can be unsavory for governments or for the military. Much has been written about the sometimes-rocky relationship between war correspondents and the military. It is absolutely essential that journalists have access to events so that they can report what's going on. However, it is becoming a concern for journalists to have access to such events because their own safety is being threatened. For instance, in the recent U.S. military action in Afghanistan, it is suspected that there was an unofficial policy in Afghanistan to target Western journalists and do them harm. Eight journalists

A Dangerous Job

Reporters Ian Stewart and Myles Tierney were two reporters who went to Sierra Leone, a country in western Africa, in 1999 to cover the events of the country's civil war. The war had been going on for ten years, and both reporters had been to Sierra Leone on several occasions to cover the war. Both had asked to return. However, for Myles Tierney, it would be the final trip.

On the way to the scene of rebel troops closing in on the country's capital, Freetown, the car in which they were riding was ambushed. Stewart was shot in the head but, miraculously, recovered in a hospital in London. Myles Tierney was killed instantly.

Myles Tierney is shown here in 1997. During an assignment in the African nation of Sierra Leone in 1999, he was tragically shot and killed during a rebel attack.

were killed in the line of duty in Afghanistan in late 2001 covering the U.S. invasion, according to the CPJ.

Overview of the Skills Needed for the Job

For those people who make war correspondence their career, the positives far outweigh the negatives. Naturally, the risks of the job are significant. You are putting your life on the line and facing danger on a constant basis. You need plenty of courage and an ability to think quickly under pressure. How would you deal with trying to get a story from a person pointing a gun at you? You need to have an ability to rough it, to do without some modern conveniences. You have to have a strong stomach. You may be seeing violent scenes and wounded people. You'll probably be eating local cuisine, which may be different from anything else that you've ever put in your mouth.

To be a good war correspondent, you need courage, compassion, good writing skills, and inquisitiveness. It's a plus if you know how to influence people and how

French television journalist Corinne Gaucherand is escorted by soldiers after a government order to leave the Philippines in July 2000. The capture of three of her colleagues by Abu Sayyaf Muslim separatists prompted the order.

to be persuasive. Keep in mind that you may be interviewing people who don't especially want to talk to you. How are you going to convince them to talk to you? You can't be shy. You need the ability to be a self-starter and to be self-motivated. In war correspondence, there isn't anyone to look over your shoulder to make sure that you make your deadlines. It is a good profession for people who like to travel and who like to work independently. You need to know about the technology needed to file stories; you should be computer literate, because video phones and laptop computers are important tools of the trade. Not only do you have to have a good command of the English language, it also wouldn't hurt to know at least one other language.

Getting Started in the Business 2

If you've decided that a career in war correspondence might be for you, there is plenty that you can do right now, while you are still in school, to prepare yourself for this exciting, demanding profession. You can read and write. You can submit articles to your local newspaper. You can work on your school newspaper, yearbook, or literary magazine. You can study a foreign language. You can hone your computer skills. You can practice interviewing skills by interviewing your friends and family. It wouldn't hurt to take a few photography courses, either. As a photojournalist, you'll have two talents that potential employers could want—photography and reporting. Do you see how much

Working on a school newspaper, like these students at Johnston High School in Austin, Texas, can help you prepare for a real career in journalism later on.

you can do to jumpstart your career as a war correspondent? What are you waiting for? Get going!

Reading Between the Lines

The first thing you can do is read. It is through reading, especially through reading literature, that you will gain proficiency with the English language. Reading will help you to become a good writer, and reading literature is more fun than reading grammar books, but you get the same skill. Reading can also help you to stay informed about a wide variety of subjects. You never know when a certain bit of trivia might provide the clue to cracking a news story. Read newspapers and news magazines to see the way that the news is reported. Read several different newspapers to see the way the news is reported in each one.

Can you detect a bias in the way the news is reported in newspapers? A bias is when a story takes a certain slant, or presents one side of an issue more favorably than other sides. Journalists, and news media, are supposed to remain unbiased. However, that is a difficult thing to do. Many factors influence the biases that creep into a newspaper, not the least of which are the preferences of the writers, the editors, the publishers, and the advertisers.

The book *Flash! The Associated Press Covers the World* explains what many take as the guideline of journalistic writing. Lawrence Gobright, the first AP Washington, D.C., correspondent, wrote during the United States Civil War: "My business is to communicate facts; my instructions do not allow me to make any comment upon the facts that I communicate . . . my dispatches are merely dry matters of fact and detail." However, even reporting "just the facts" can sometimes get journalists into hot water. For instance, the U.S. military and government officials were outraged that some reporters in Vietnam were writing articles that did not flat-out support what the United States was doing in Vietnam. But objective reporting enabled Americans to see what was really happening during the Vietnam War, and the horror Americans witnessed eventually led to the end of the conflict.

If you know that you'd like to cover a specific type of journalism, you should read magazines and newspapers that report that type of news. Reading good literature can also help your writing. You can read books about history, sociology, political science, or current events to help you understand the world about which you'll be writing as a war correspondent. For instance, if you are interested in the plight of women living under the burqa, the head-to-toe garment that women are forced to wear in some Muslim nations, pay special attention to the way such issues are reported in the news. You might also read the history of the Taliban, the Islamic group that was in power in

Betsey Halstead is shown here in military gear coming home in 1965 after covering the Vietnam War in Saigon for United Press International. At twenty-three years old, she was one of the youngest foreign correspondents at the time, and one of only a handful of female correspondents.

Afghanistan, or about the treatment of women in Saudi Arabia. To write good news stories, you need to be informed about history as well as about current events. Read style manuals such as the *Chicago Manual of Style*, the *AP Style Guide*, and *Strunk and White's Elements of Style* to polish up your grammar and newswriting skills.

Brush Up on Your Writing

The second thing you can do right now to prepare yourself for a career in war correspondence is to write. Write e-mails or letters to friends and family. Write editorials to the local newspaper. You could try submitting articles to newspapers on a freelance basis. That means that you come up with an idea for stories and then write and submit the articles yourself instead of having an editor hire you to write an article about a specific subject. That also means that you might not get paid at first for these articles, or that you might be paid very little for them. When you are beginning your career as a reporter, the important thing is getting your work published, not whether you get paid for what you've published.

How do you write freelance articles? Start by noticing if there are any events going on in your town, such as parades, fairs, town council meetings, or the openings of new businesses. Then get yourself to these events. Observe the events and record what is happening. Try to interview the key people involved with the event by explaining to them that you are writing an article about the event and that you will be submitting it to the local newspaper. Many event organizers welcome the chance to talk to reporters because a newspaper article is good, free publicity. But don't represent yourself as working for a publication if you do not actually work for it.

It is a good idea to keep a daily journal. Even writing for fifteen minutes a day will help you get used to expressing your ideas in writing. Above all, good writing skills are the tools a war correspondent needs most. There are too many other factors you will have to worry about once you are at the scene of a battle, so concentrate on your writing skills now. At the scene of a conflict, you could be scurrying around, ducking bombs or gunfire. It is no time to be

You May Have Heard Of...

Many prominent writers and journalists got their start in war reporting, among them Edward R. Murrow, Jack London, Rudyard Kipling, Winston Churchill, Ernest Hemingway, Al Gore, Walter Cronkite, and Dan Rather.

Dan Rather, pictured here in Somalia in 1992, is one of many reporters who broke into journalism through war correspondence.

searching for the perfect adjective or sentence structure. You want to make sure that your writing skills are absolutely solid before you ever get to the front lines.

Work at a Newspaper

You can try to get a job at your local newspaper. The competition will not be as stiff at small-town publications as it will be at big city newspapers. Even if you are not asked to write your own column right away (and there is a good chance that you will not be asked to do that right away), it will be extremely helpful for you to work on a newspaper, no matter what you do there. Even if you are selling advertising for the paper, if you keep your eyes and ears open at the office, you can learn a lot about the newspaper business. Everyone has to work his or her way up from somewhere. Some of the most famous journalists, including people like Walter Cronkite, had to pay their dues before they got a shot at being an anchorperson. Working at the paper will help you gain experience and meet people who could help you get a better job after you have a college degree.

If your school has a newspaper, a literary magazine, or even a yearbook, get yourself on the staff. If your school does not have these publications, you may want to consider asking a teacher or the principal if you can start one.

A scene from the film *Almost Famous*, in which a teenager-turned-rock reporter, William Miller (Patrick Fugit, right), asks advice from his mentor, famed music journalist Lester Bangs, played by Philip Seymour Hoffman

College: To Major in Journalism or Not?

Many people who have gone on to become war correspondents majored in journalism, while others studied liberal arts subjects such as history, English literature, or political science. Having a degree in journalism does not ensure that you will get a reporting job quicker than if you had a degree in a liberal arts subject, so you should major in what you are drawn to. There are many schools where you could concentrate just on journalism. Journalism courses differ depending on the kind of news you'd like to do. If you want to work for a newspaper or a magazine, you may not need the radio broadcasting or video courses you'd have to take if you wanted to get a job in television news.

As a journalism major, you will take general courses in newswriting, editing, and photography, as well as classes that cover the history of journalism and the laws or ethics of reporting. The rest of your courses will be liberal arts courses such as English, history, political science, sociology, and economics. You may also be required to take some general math and science courses.

As a journalism major, you may also take advanced courses in the finer points of writing, reporting, and editing. You'll take classes that cover how to write feature stories or how to be an investigative reporter. There is no school in the United States, though, that prepares war correspondents for protecting themselves at the scene of a battle.

If you want some help in choosing a college, check out the list of journalism schools compiled by the Accrediting Council of Education in Journalism and Mass Communications (ACEJMC), which is certified by the United States Department of Education. High school sutdents (or their parents) can look to ACEJMC to answer questions about accredited programs. Their Web site, http://www.ku.edu/~acejmc, provides a wealth of information to help find a college that's right

Studying journalism in college or in a masters program can be helpful, but is not required to enter the field. Here, a teacher lectures at the S.I. Newhouse School of Journalism at Syracuse University, one of the most respected journalism schools in the country.

for you. This organization has strict standards of excellence, so you can be sure that any school on its list is a good one.

One last bit of advice: Try to get an internship, even if it is unpaid, which most are. Journalism is a competitive field, and many employers look for candidates with work experience as well as academic excellence. Get all of the experience you can.

War Correspondents Past and Present

Reports differ on when exactly the first official war correspondence occurred. The fact of the matter is that whenever and wherever people have taken up arms, war correspondents have been there. People seem to have a never-ending fascination with war. War is an event in which so much is at stake. There are many opportunities for courage and there are just as many chances to make mistakes that could be spectacular errors. Thanks to war correspondents, not all of the events of war are conducted in secrecy. This is both a blessing and a curse to the participants. War correspondence at its best sometimes ensures that acts of bravery do not go unnoticed or that terrible events can eventually be revealed and corrected. However, there is a delicate balance between telling what needs to be told and making public information that could harm troops. For instance, you can imagine how battle strategies being on the front pages of newspapers would completely ruin a surprise attack planned by troops.

A Brief History of War Correspondence

There are several factors involved in the birth of professional war correspondence. One is a free press. Government officials allowed war correspondents because they wanted reporters to champion democracy. Time was another factor. For example, during the Crimean War (1853–1856), the English wanted more news more quickly than the participants of the war could supply. The Crimean War was a war fought by England, France, and the Ottoman Turks against Russia. The war was about Russia's claim to Palestinian holy places. The *London Times* sent

War Correspondents: Life Under Fire

William Howard Russell to the front. He was called a war correspondent because he did indeed write letters about the war for the *Times*. Another factor contributing to the birth of war correspondence is the growth of technology. This technological growth enhanced the speed of correspondence, which intensified the competition for war correspondents to have the first and most accurate dispatches from the front.

For centuries, the participants of war, the soldiers, were the ones who were doing the war reporting. We

William Howard Russell (1820–1907) was a British war correspondent who covered several conflicts, including the Crimean War and the U.S. Civil War.

know what went on in ancient Roman battles thanks to the letters of people such as Roman emperor Julius Caesar. The one advantage that soldier-correspondents had over the war correspondents of today is that the soldiers did not have to worry about being barred from the scene of battle—they were already on the scene. The modern war correspondent has to contend with restricted access to the scene of conflict in a way that has never been known before. This is because during conflicts such as in Afghanistan, hostile groups have targeted journalists, wishing to harm them.

According to *Crimes of War*, war correspondents must be accredited by the military with which they are going to the scene of battle. During some wars, correspondents wore uniforms that were similar to, but not identical to, the uniforms worn by the military forces about which they were writing. In the early 1960s, war correspondents still wore army-issue fatigues, but by 1970, war correspondents in Vietnam were wearing civilian clothes. War correspondents used to run the risk of being shot as spies, until the 1949 Geneva Convention set in writing the protection of war correspondents. But there is still the risk of being captured by enemy forces. It is unlikely that all enemy forces know that violence to war correspondents

The Geneva Convention, shown here being signed in December 1949, is recognized by most nations around the world and expressly prohibits violence against war correspondents, among other rules of war.

is against the Geneva Convention! Daniel Pearl's killers either didn't know, or simply didn't care.

Famous War Correspondents

The *World Book Encyclopedia* claims that George W. Kendall, founder of the *New Orleans Picayune*, (now the *Times-Picayune*) was the first to set up a system of messengers to speed the news of the Mexican War

Christiane Amanpour

Christiane Amanpour is CNN's chief international correspondent based in London. Throughout the 1990s, she worked in hot spots such as Iran, Afghanistan, Bosnia, and Rwanda, reporting from the scenes of conflict. In fact, no U.S. correspondent has reported from Bosnia as consistently as Amanpour has. She was largely responsible for bringing the situation in Bosnia to the U.S. public's attention. In September 2001, she conducted a live, exclusive interview with Pakistani president General Pervez Musharraf about his country's position after the September, 11, 2001, terrorist attacks on the World Trade Center in New York City and the Pentagon in Washington, D.C.

For her reporting from the former Yugoslavia, Amanpour received a News and Documentary Emmy Award, two George Foster Peabody Awards, a George Polk Award, a Courage in Journalism Award, a Worldfest-Houston International Film Festival Gold Award, and the Livingston Award for Young Journalists. She also was named 1994 Woman of the Year by the New York chapter of Women in Cable and Telecommunications, and she helped the CNN network win a DuPont Award for its coverage of Bosnia and a Golden CableACE for its Gulf War coverage.

Christiane Amanpour is shown receiving a Peabody Award in May 1999 for her overseas reporting, which has included stints in war-torn areas like Bosnia, Rwanda, and Afghanistan. Flanking her are Barry L. Sherman, Peabody Awards director *(left)*, and CNN president Eason Jordan.

(1846–1848) back to the United States. Some say it was during the Crimean War. William Howard Russell became a famous British war correspondent because of his coverage of Britain's role in the Crimean War. Some of Russell's dispatches concerning the lack of nurses to care for wounded soldiers led well-known nurse Florence Nightingale to organize a nursing corps to support British troops in the Crimea.

Russell was also noted for his coverage of the U.S. Civil War (1861–1865). By the time the Civil War in

America was being fought, war correspondents had become established pieces of the landscape of war. Freelance correspondent Mark Kellogg was the first Associated Press correspondent to die in battle. He was killed covering General George Custer at the Battle of Little Bighorn on June 25, 1876. Since that time, there have been many famous war correspondents, among them Marguerite Higgins (1920–1966), who was the first woman to win the Pulitzer Prize for international reporting for her coverage of the Korean War (1950–1953). Ernest Taylor Pyle (1900–1945) was a war correspondent whose reports from the front lines in Europe during World War II brought much-needed information about the war to the anxious families waiting at home. He was shot and killed by a Japanese soldier in 1945.

Women War Correspondents: Some Highlights

On the back cover of Phillip Knightley's critically acclaimed book, *The First Casualty*, there are twelve

War Correspondents: Life Under Fire

pictures of famous war correspondents, and each one is a picture of a man. It may come as no surprise to you to learn that there have been, and there continue to be, many women war correspondents whose work has won distinguished awards and whose writing was extremely important to many civilians. During Franklin Delano Roosevelt's tenure as president of the United States, First Lady Eleanor Roosevelt started a weekly women-only press conference to force news organizations to hire at least one female reporter.

Famous war correspondent Marguerite Higgins, shown here on a military transport plane in 1956, won a Pulitzer Prize for her earlier coverage of the Korean War.

During World War II, many of the newswomen in the first lady's circle served as war correspondents. The rich history of women war correspondents includes:

◆ Dickey Chapelle (1919–1965), a war correspondent and photographer, was killed by a booby trap in the Vietnam conflict. She had been a war correspondent for twenty-three years and was the first American woman journalist killed in action.

◆ Margaret Fuller (1810–1850) was the *New York Herald Tribune*'s European correspondent in the 1840s. In 1844, Horace Greeley hired Fuller as a literary critic. She was the *New York Herald Tribune*'s first female staff member, and she went to Europe in 1848 to cover the European revolutions that were occurring.

◆ Peggy Hull (1889–1967), on September 17, 1918, won accreditation from the U.S. Department of War to become the first official American female war correspondent. She went on to serve as a correspondent during World War II.

War Correspondents: Life Under Fire

◆ Dorothy Thompson (1894–1961) was the Berlin correspondent for the *New York Evening Post* in the 1930s. Her reporting about the Nazi movement infuriated Adolf Hitler so much that, by his own personal order in 1934, she became the first American correspondent to be expelled from Germany.

The Future
of War
Correspondence

4

As you can imagine, innovations in communications and information technology are changing the face of journalism and, therefore, changing the prospects for war correspondents. Because it costs so much money for the media to have the latest equipment, it is not always possible for media companies to afford full-time coverage of international news. Only the largest corporations that own newspapers, television stations, and radio stations can afford that kind of coverage. This could mean one of two things for those who want to be war correspondents. You could become extremely knowledgeable in a certain field, increasing your chances of being hired because you will beat out the competition in that portion of international news by doing better reports. Or, you can decide to be a freelance reporter, also called a stringer. Those media companies that cannot afford full-time correspondents are increasingly relying on freelance reporters. That's good news for you if being a freelance war correspondent sounds appealing.

Smaller publications like the *Jersey Journal* are good places to gain valuable news experience before you attempt to cover foreign conflicts. Here, the staff celebrates in February 2002 after the paper was saved from shutting down due to cutbacks and labor disputes.

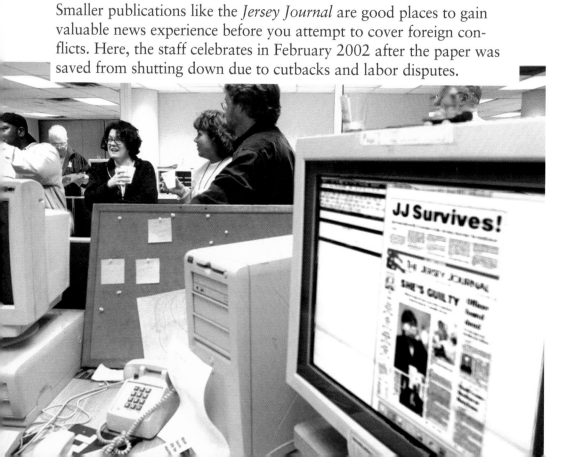

Job Outlook

The *Occupational Outlook Handbook* 2002–2003 edition groups correspondents with news analysts and reporters, so it is difficult to get an entirely accurate picture of how many war correspondents are working today, and what the demand for their services will be in the future. According to the handbook, news analysts, reporters, and correspondents held about 78,000 jobs in the United States in 2000. Nearly half worked for newspapers—either large city dailies or suburban and small town dailies or weeklies. About 28 percent worked in radio and television broadcasting, and others worked for magazines and wire services. About 12,000 news analysts, reporters, and correspondents were self-employed.

Employment for reporters and correspondents is expected to increase from 3 to 9 percent. This modest increase is due to the fact that many companies are merging, creating fewer publications and fewer jobs. Some increases can be expected in television and radio jobs, as well as online newspapers and magazines. There will still be a lot of competition for jobs on large metropolitan newspapers, broadcast stations, and national magazines. Writers who demonstrate a talent for writing about highly specialized scientific or technical subjects have an advantage. Also, newspapers increasingly are hiring stringers and freelancers. This is in part because many publications cannot afford to have full-time correspondents. Only the biggest publications can afford such a staff.

Most entry-level openings will be for jobs at small publications. This is because reporters and correspondents at smaller publications usually become either editors or reporters on larger publications, or leave the field. Small town and suburban newspapers will continue to be the best places to cut your teeth in the field of journalism.

Earnings

Salaries for correspondents vary. In general, they are relatively high, except at small stations and small publications, where salaries often are very low. Correspondents earned an average of $29,110 per year in 2000. The middle 50 percent earned between

$21,320 and $45,540. The lowest 10 percent earned less than $16,540, while the highest 10 percent earned more than $69,300. In radio and television broadcasting, correspondents earned an average of $33,550 per year in 2000. In newspapers, correspondents earned an average of $26,900 per year in 2000.

According to a 1999 survey conducted by the National Association of Broadcasters and the Broadcast Cable Financial Management Association, the annual average salary, including bonuses, was $83,400 per year for weekday anchors and $44,200 for those working on weekends. Television news reporters earned on average $33,700 per year. Weekday sportscasters typically earned $68,900, while weekend sportscasters earned $37,200. Weathercasters averaged $68,500 during the week and $36,500 on weekends. According to the 2001 survey, the annual average salary for radio news reporters, including bonuses, was $55,100.

Less to Tell?

Aside from the more particular questions of job prospects and salaries, it is not so easy to predict the future for war correspondents with regard to the way that they go about doing their exciting but dangerous jobs. It would seem that the tension that has existed between the military and the media, which dates at least from the Vietnam War, still exists to the degree that war correspondents are getting less and less access to battle scenes. It is perhaps frustrating to imagine that in a technological age, in which the Internet and satellite transmissions allow correspondents to send live footage directly from the front lines, there might be fewer chances for a reporter to be there.

Phillip Knightley, in a March 20, 2000, article in the *Guardian*, put it this way, "What had changed between Vietnam and Kosovo? Basically, the military has won its 150-year battle with war correspondents: journalists want to tell the public everything; the military's attitude is: 'Tell them nothing till the war's over, then tell them who won.'" According to a December 4, 2001, article by Kim Campbell in the *Christian Science Monitor*, "Other changes have occurred in war reporting since the tanks rolled into Kuwait— advances in the form of satellite and video phones, and obstacles, in the form of more limited access to

A cameraman readies his tripod to begin filming television coverage of a refugee camp for Rwandans in Bukavu, Zaire, after prolonged bloodshed in Rwanda prompted many of its citizens to flee.

the battlefield. Now, say observers, reporters can deliver news from war zones in real time, but they have less to tell."

It is difficult for war correspondents to counter such tactics from the military. Because of the danger involved in their work, war correspondents have short working lives and there is no system, no tradition, for war correspondents to give each other the tricks of the trade. The military, on the other hand, has plenty of systems for passing along information about how the military should deal with the press.

Risk Assessment

As a result of the terrorist attacks of September 11, 2001, companies such as Centurion Risk Assessment Services are seeing an increase in the demand for their services. These companies teach people how to cope in a hostile environment. Centurion has taught 7,000 journalists since it first opened its doors for business in 1995. The company offers training at its Hampshire, England, location and also offers on-location training.

Some of its clients have included journalists from the British Broadcasting Corporation (the BBC), the *New York Times*, Reuters, and the television networks ABC and NBC. The course includes the operation of weapons, what to do if you get kidnapped or captured, how to recognize and avoid land mines and booby traps, and emergency first aid, such as how to stop someone from bleeding to death. Courses in chemical and biological warfare have recently been added.

As you have found out by reading this book, a career in war correspondence can be extremely rewarding. It is a challenging and a stimulating job, one that could get you quite a bit of recognition. Even better than the idea of winning a Pulitzer Prize or getting your name and face on television broadcasts is the knowledge that you are providing a vital service to your fellow citizens. The press is the watchdog of society. It is through the efforts of journalists that the public understands whether or not its needs are being served by its government. War correspondence is a field that involves serious risks, too. Not many employers are going to encourage their workers to risk their lives to get a story. However, if you want to be a war correspondent, it's part of the job description. You need to be where the conflict is. Ironically, one of the challenges you will face as a war correspondent is the risk that the story you have endangered your life to write will end up being censored. It could sit forever in a file in a room at the Pentagon in Washington, D.C., and never reach a newspaper, where it can inform the public.

But in spite of all of the danger, you're hooked. You want to become a war correspondent. Will you try to get a full-time job at a news agency such as the Associated Press or Reuters? Does being part of a weekly or a daily newspaper staff appeal to you? Perhaps you are the independent type and would like to be a freelance correspondent. There are many paths that you could take to achieve your goal. Only one thing is certain. There is a whole world out there waiting for you.

Glossary

accredited To be recognized by an organization as having a certain set of credentials.

Associated Press (AP) A news agency that sells news items to the print and broadcast media.

bias A preference toward one thing over another.

casualty Something that has come to an end or someone who has died.

censor When a person or an organization tells you what you can and can't write about.

dailies Publications that get published every day.

deadline The point in time at which a correspondent's story must be completed and sent to his or her editor.

dispatches Messages written by foreign correspondents.

improvising Thinking quickly to make things up as you go along.

War Correspondents: Life Under Fire

inquisitiveness Curiosity.

news briefings Meetings held by the military or the government to inform the media about battles, wars, or conflicts in which the government or the military is involved.

proactive Assertive in getting what you want.

Pulitzer Prize One of the highest achievements in journalism in the United States.

satellite A man-made object in space that circles Earth.

suburban Outside of the city, but not too far outside of it.

Taliban The fundamentalist Muslim group that was in power in Afghanistan.

weeklies Publications that get published every week.

For More Information

American Society of Journalists and Authors
1501 Broadway, Suite 302
New York, NY 10036
(212) 997-0947
Web site: http://www.asja.org

American Society of Magazine Editors
919 Third Avenue, 22nd Floor
New York, NY 10022
(212) 872-3700
Web site: http://asme.magazine.org

American Society of Newspaper Editors
11690B Sunrise Valley Drive
Reston, VA 20131-1409
(703) 453-1122
Web site: http://www.asne.org

War Correspondents: Life Under Fire

Committee to Protect Journalists (CPJ)
330 Seventh Avenue, 12th floor
New York, NY 10001
(212) 465-1004
Web site: http://www.cpj.org

Editorial Freelancers Association
71 West 23rd Street, Suite 1910
New York, NY 10010
(212) 929-5400
Web site: http://www.the-efa.org

Newseum: The Interactive Museum of News
1101 Wilson Boulevard
Arlington, VA 22209
Web site: http://www.newseum.org

The Poynter Institute
801 Third Street South
St. Petersburg, FL 33701
(888) 769-6837
Web site: http://www.poynter.org

Radio-Television News Directors Association
   & Foundation
1600 K Street NW, Suite 700
Washington, DC 20006-2838
(202) 659-6510
Web site: http://www.rtnda.org

Society of Professional Journalists
Eugene S. Pulliam National Journalism Center
3909 North Meridian Street
Indianapolis, IN 46208
(317) 927-8000
Web site: http://spj.org

In Canada

Periodical Writers Association of Canada
54 Wolseley Street, Suite 203
Toronto, ON M5T 1A5
(416) 504-1645
Web site: http://www.web.net/~pwac

Writers' Union of Canada
40 Wellington Street East, Third Floor
Toronto, ON M5E 1C7
(416) 703-8982
Web site: http://www.writersunion.ca

Web Sites

Due to the changing nature of Internet links, the Rosen Publishing Group, Inc., has developed an on-line list of Web sites related to the subject of this book. This site is updated regularly. Please use this link to access the list:

http://www.rosenlinks.com/ec/waco.html

For Further Reading

Colman, Penny. *Where the Action Was: Women War Correspondents in World War II.* New York: Crown Publishers, 2002.

Emery, Michael. *On the Front Lines: Following America's Foreign Correspondents Across the Twentieth Century.* Washington, D.C.: American University Press, 1995.

Gruber, Ruth. *Ahead of Time: My Early Years as a Foreign Correspondent.* New York: Carroll & Graf Publishers, Incorporated, 2001.

Hess, Stephen. *International News and Foreign Correspondents.* Washington, D.C.: Brookings Institution Press, 1996.

Kaplan, Andrew. *Careers for Wordsmiths.* Brookfield, CT: Millbrook Press, Inc., 1991.

War Correspondents: Life Under Fire

O'Conner, Barbara. *The Soldiers' Voice: The Story of Ernie Pyle.* Minneapolis, MN: The Lerner Publishing Group, 1996.

Stein, M.L. *Under Fire: The Story of American War Correspondents.* Parsippany, NJ: Silver Burdett Press, 1995.

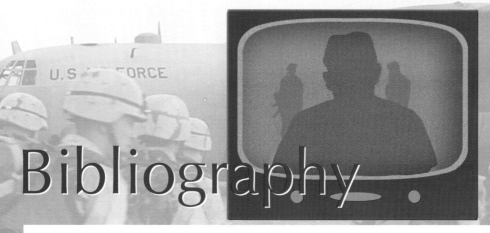

Bibliography

Goldberg, Jan. *Careers in Journalism.* Chicago: VGM
   Career Horizons, 1999.

Knightley, Philip. *The First Casualty: The War
   Correspondent as Hero and Myth-Maker from the
   Crimea to Kosovo.* Baltimore, MD: Johns Hopkins
   University Press, 2002.

Zoeller, Chuck, Vincent Alabiso, and Kelly Smith-
   Tunney. *Flash! The Associated Press Covers the
   World.* New York: Harry N. Abrams,
   Incorporated, 1998.

Index

About the Author

Magdalena Alagna is an editor and writer living in New York City.

Photo Credits

Cover © Dennis Brack/Department of Defense (DOD)/Timepix; pp. 5, 15, 38, 44 © AP/Wide World Photos; pp. 7, 11 © Reuters NewMedia Inc./Corbis; pp. 13, 17 © AFP/Corbis; p. 20 © Bob Daemmrich/The Image Works; pp. 23, 34, 36, 40 © Bettmann/ Corbis; p. 26 © Peter Tunnley/Corbis; p. 28 © The Everett Collection; p. 30 © Dick Blume, Charles Jackson/The Image Works; p. 49 © Howard Davies/Corbis.

Series Design

Les Kanturek

Layout

Tahara Hasan